Listen!

Wisdom from the Heart of a Poetess

Doris Dean Hannah Turner

LISTEN! Wisdom from the Heart of a Poetess
Copyright © 2022 by Doris Dean Hannah Turner
ISBN 978-1-7362277-4-9 (Paperback)
ISBN 978-1-7362277-5-6 (Hardcover)

Designed and Published by King's Daughter Publishing
Indian Trail, North Carolina 28079
www.KingsDaughterPublishing.com

All rights reserved. No part of this publication may be reproduced, stored in a retrieval system or transmitted, in any form or by any means, electronic, mechanical, photocopying, recording or otherwise, without permission in writing from the author.

Printed in the United States of America.

Table of Contents

Dedication	7
Acknowledgements	9
The Grand Canyon	10
Who Are You, Black Child?	11
Faith of a Mustard Seed	13
Judgemental Arses	14
Birthing Through the Pain	15
Breakthrough	16
Inside Your Head	17
Before I Rise	18
One	19
The Change is Within You	20
Dawdling in Stew	21
A Safe Place	22
The Dawn of a New Day	23
Golden Blessings	24
A Winding Staircase	25
I am Transparent	26
This Filly is Free	27
Dreams of Youth	29
Embrace Yourself	30
Listen!	31
Quality of Life	32
Generational Knowledge	33
Firefly, Firefly	34
Fresh Start	35
One Hell of a Man	36
The Most High	37
In the Beginning	39
Rites of Passage	40
A Father's Heart	41
Duck!	42

Boon-Docks	43
Eternal Rest	45
Heart 2 Heart (In Memory of Pauletta)	46
If I Had Known	47
The Warrior	48
Becoming Vegan	49
The Unsung Hero	50
Archiving Memories	51
The Third Age	52
Spokes on the Wheel of Life	53
Everlasting Prayer	54
Chosen by Heart	55
Pearl	56
Blood Bond	57
Quadripartite	58
My God is Brilliant	59
Joy, Real Joy	60
Proud Heritage	61
My Heart Belongs to Africa	62
The Comforter	63
Conception	64
The Front Row	65
Sibling Squabbles	66
A Little Bit of Heaven (Trim Pines)	67
True Gem	68
Ancestral Heritage	69
Church Family	70
Global Pandemic of 2020	71
Essential Rules	73
The Chambers of Eve's Heart	74
Spring in the Southern Hemisphere	75
Accumulator	76
The Wings of Championship	77
In My Mother's Dwelling	78
Wajukuu (Grandchildren)	80

Irresistible	81
A Butterfly Trapped in Honey	82
A Father's Ballad	84
Transitioning	85
Wisdom from Persephone	86
I Am That Woman	87
Love Incarnate	88
Expressions of a Poet	90
Love Prevails	91
Cabaret Waltz	92
Infinite Love	93
Reckoning	94
Tiara the Fascinator	95
House of Haven	96
Journey of My Weight in Time	97
Message to My Sistahs	99
Tribute to Mama Whiteside	101
Life Ingredients	103
Essence of a First Lady	104
My Pen, My Paper, My Poetry	105
About the Author	107

Dedication

...

I would like to dedicate this book to my children and their spouses, Michael Jr. (Lori), Samuel (Cencelia), and Phyllis (Charo I).

To my Grandchildren—Lauren and Domanic Wilson, I, Eboni, Charo II, Codee and Caree.

My Great Grandchildren—E'lani, Kloee, and Domanic, II.

To you, and to future generations, I write to leave you a legacy.

My Siblings—Johnny Hannah, Annette Tinsley, and Rachel Woods, who are not a season but permanent in my life. I love you.

You are my reason.

Acknowledgements

...

My Nieces—Alesada Colon' and Julia Turner Lindell, for titling some of my poetry and inspiring me to think creatively.

My Friends—Regina Horton and Reva Binion Henry, for their input. Cousin Marlon Hannah who is always there to make sure I don't fall. Rashida LaShawn Williams, The Collaborative by T & G for glam & photography. Publisher, S. Kristi Douglas, who is anointed by God for her creative talent.

Family and friends who have inspired me to write about them for whatever reason. Without you, "Listen!" wouldn't exist.

The Grand Canyon
...

The feminine and masculine characteristics
Are what I see.

Her statuesque beauty has an array of colors
You can see from afar.

She covers many miles
As you look upon her from the sky.

Her layers are many as she continues
To birth plenty.

As she matures, she ages to perfection.
She glows from every angle of her massive being.

She captivates everyone who sets eyes upon her.

The masculine side of this magnificent foundation is
Rough and rugged with sharp edges from side to side.

His foundation is something you can lean on because
He's very strong.

Made from many different chunks
And built like a hunk.

He's wide like a river that will continue to flow.

His pure existence has captivated millions of people
From near and far.

Though he's ancient, he will stand for many years.

So, no matter what characteristics you see—
Feminine or masculine...

It's a beauty and a wonder to behold from the naked eye.

Who Are You, Black Child?

Who are you, black child?
Who might you become?

Always have a dream.
Keep yourself focused
On who you can become.

Who are you, black child?
Who might you become?

Must you play video games or
Stay on your phone all day long?

Have you considered becoming
An inventor of video games, or
An owner of a company?

Who are you, black child?
Who might you become?

Must you play music all day long?

Play if you must; but have you
Considered becoming a poet,
A novelist or a composer of music
Of some kind?

Who are you, black child?
Who might you become?

You want tattoos all over your body.
Consider becoming a doctor of medicine
Or a nurse.

Study and stay in school.
Stop complaining that your teacher doesn't like you.

She has her degree.
Get what you must.
Don't be lazy in the process.
Knowledge is the key to success.

The struggle was real in the past.
They paved the way for your success.

Achieve the task and make yourself
Proud of who you are
And who you can become.

Who are you, black child?

You are a child of the King.
Yes! Black child.
That is who you are!

Faith of a Mustard Seed
...

You must visualize
Before you can achieve.

Put your mind in check to
Accomplish what you believe.

Your way of thinking is like a
Disease infecting your mind
And crippling your inner being.

Focus on the positive and
Just believe.

Judgemental Arses

Your opinion is a judgement
Which I don't care to hear.

Will it uplift my spirit, or cause me despair?

You are not my judge nor my jury
So why should I care?

Do you want unwanted advice
Creeping up in your life?

No matter how big or small,
Your advice should stay in your thoughts.
It's not meant to express to all.

I have weathered the storms of my life
And defeated the challenges
The devil has tried to cast upon me.

So, I own the right to manage my own life
Without your judgmental advice.

When you have walked in my shoes
Maybe you can give me your advice.

The next time you have an opinion,
Keep it to yourself.
Figure out how to handle your own tests of life.

Let's keep it real.
Focus on your life.
Because I don't need your judgmental advice.

Birthing Through the Pain
...

Don't allow challenges to cause you
Pain and strife throughout your life.

Push through and ask God to deliver you.

Going through the tests of life gives you
Experience and you learn endurance.

Remember, it's up to you to make a change.
Take your mistakes and turn them into life lessons
Never to repeat again.

Life is a challenge, I'm sure you know.
So never give up on life no matter what it takes.

Because birthing takes place
After pushing through the pain.

Breakthrough

When you feel down and blue,
Look for ways to bless others,
It takes the focus off of you.

Whatever your talent may be,
Make use of it to put a smile on someone's face.
It will brighten up their day.

Don't just stand there and be blue.
Continue to bless until you get a
Breakthrough.

Bless until those feelings turn into joy.

In the midst of blessing someone else,
You will be blessed, too.

Inside Your Head
...

A poem comes from inside your head.
Relax and let it spread.

It takes a moment to get deep into it.
Just meditate and let it develop inside your head.

You might be amazed by the talent you possess.
Let your soul flow into it.

Just be still and let The Almighty work
As you step into it.

Don't be afraid, just relax.

And before you know it,
It has already developed
Inside your head.

Before I Rise
...

Before I rise, my soul lies in wait
Searching for words to say.

My heart starts to beat
Like the sound of an African drum
From within my soul.

Words begin to form into poetry
And start to flow.

They challenge me
And I'm ready to deliver
From the gut of my soul.

Poems of wisdom,
Poems of love.
Poems of encouragement.
Rising above.

Poems about my heritage and
The places I have been.

So, before you rise at the dawn
Of a new day,
Lie still and let the words bubble up
And take control.

You never know what might be
Rising from within your soul.

One
...

He created a magnificent being in you.
Be kind and true to the one and only body
God has given you.

One body, soul and spirit.
Be careful how you treat it.

You only get one body.
One soul.
And one spirit.

The Change is Within You

The change is within you.
You have to start somewhere.

No matter what stage of life you're in
No more brooding over what could've been.

So, stop it!

It's you who are stopping yourself from
What you need to do.

Pick up your life from where you are.
Focus, it is within you.

The past no longer matters.
Your future is in your hands.

Now what do you plan to do?

Don't look back.
Don't feed negativity.
It will only destroy you.

Age doesn't matter
As long as you believe.

Be persistent; don't give up.
You can do it!

Turn that "could've" into reality
It's in your destiny.

Become true to YOU.

Dawdling in Stew
. . .

Stop procrastinating.
It ain't cute.

Get off your rump and
Stop letting it consume you.

Days, hours and weeks have passed by.
It's blocking your creativity
That's bottled up inside you.

Or, maybe something else has a grip on you.

Depression.
Fear.
Is that stopping you?

Just stop procrastinating.
Every day find a way.
Don't let it consume you.

A Safe Place
...

Where is a safe place in your space?
It may be in your home all alone.

Or, creating your own zone.

In your mind, let it unwind.

By meditating or just having
A glass of wine.

A safe place is where you make it.

Take some time off and create it—
That safe place for yourself.

You might be amazed to find that safe place
In front of your face.

The Dawn of a New Day

As the dawn of a new day breaks through
I can see the heavens and
Hear life and nature surrounding me.

The birds are singing and chirping.
They are excited for the start of a new day.

The male birds are singing.
They are protecting their territory.
They are letting the others know
They are still strong and healthy.

The deer begin to awaken,
Seeking food among their surroundings.

The squirrels are in the trees.
They seem to be looking at me.

The groundhog is hiding under my car,
Trying to get cozy and warm.

The little chipmunks are moving fast
In the cracks under my cement steps.

I suspect they are busy building a burrow of
Tunnels underneath.

The trees are very peaceful and still.

Bunnies are hopping and gazing at my veggies.
But...I'm no fool.
They better look somewhere else
Before they become rabbit stew!

In the wee hours of the morning
You can see and hear nature moving.

Just keep still.
When you see the dawn of a new day breaking through,
You will be able to see and hear all of this too.

Golden Blessings
...

If you are fortunate to have
A Senior in your life,
Count them a blessing by
Allowing them to be a part.

They are here for a reason,
With lots of wisdom to invest into your children.

Don't let a day go by.
Just spread the love
In every way, every day.

If they are prayerful and listen,
Invite them to pray for what's ailing you.

Sometimes they feel lonely.
Visitors don't come to knock
On their door anymore.

Just keep living.
Remember you may get there someday.

So, treat them with respect in every way—
The way you would like to be treated
Someday.

A Winding Staircase
...

Sometimes our lives are like
A winding staircase that has no end.

When you make a turn,
You're not sure if it's going
To be sunshine or rain.

When you see the blessing
In whatever the case,
It's how you manage in the midst of the pain.

Keep the faith and never give up.

Focusing on the positive will keep you sane
Until it's sunshine and not rain.

That winding staircase you thought would never end...

Keep the faith and you will find out
It does have an end.

I am Transparent
...

I am transparent. Yes, I am!
From the top of my head
To the tip of my toes.

Sometimes I embarrass my children
Because I talk about life with freedom
Because I think it's best.

I realize that transparency can be
Deliverance for setting someone else free.

Trials and tests in life
Are not ours to keep.

You were delivered to
Share your testimony with someone else.

So be transparent.
Tell your story.

It will be freedom for someone else.

This Filly is Free

...

My mother tried to break me
Because I was so wild and free.

She wanted to mold me
Like the potter's clay
To what she wanted me to be.

I believe she said, "This filly is too wild for me.
But I will discipline her accordingly."

Being young and silly,
I always made mistakes.

I would always get a whipping
With the tree branch
From across the woods
On Oakley Street.

And still, she couldn't mold me
Into what she wanted me to be.

No matter how many times I got a whipping,
I still broke free;
Because she didn't know
How to deal with me.

She was just doing what came to her naturally.
My spirit couldn't be broken
Because God created me.

She should have asked the Master,
His plan on how to handle me.

It could have saved her a lot of trouble
Chastising me
Because my spirit was so wild and free.

She didn't know what to do.
I felt like she was
Trying to handle my stubbornness.
But I still kept my integrity.
I was certainly not like
The other children in our family.

So, one day,
God saved my soul from eternal hell
And that wild spirit came out of me.
Deliverance is what broke and molded me.

It wasn't the switch,
But it was God's grace that kept me.
It was the key to eternity
And to be free.

Dreams of Youth
. . .

If only I was young again,
I would learn how
To bop and spin.

But now my knees feel weak and thin.
Oh man, if only I was young again.

I would bungee jump.
Go water skiing.
Rock climbing, white water rafting or
Whatever felt exciting to me.

It takes younger knees to bend,
To climb, and
To move very fast.

If only I was young again,
I would explore life's options
All over again.

Oh, who am I kidding?
Yes! Only me.

I wasn't that courageous
Even when I was young
Way back then.

I will make the best of life's opportunities
Until the very end.

Embrace Yourself

Embrace yourself.
You are beautiful in every way.

Your hair may be super course, thin or silky straight.
Don't be afraid to show your natural beauty within.

Your complexion may come in an array of shades.
Embrace yourself. You are who God made.

Your nose may be wide or narrow.
Your breasts might be large or small.
No matter what size,
It will supply the need.

Your lips might be plump like a peach or very thin.

Your butt might be booty-licious or nice and flat.
But that's okay—be satisfied with that.

You might have turkey thighs or chicken thighs.
Embrace yourself and stop complaining.

You might be bow-legged or walk with a limp.
Your feet may be long or wide but that's nothing to hide.
Your feet might be a children's size.
But remember those feet are able to take you for a ride.

All of us have what we feel are flaws,
But God made you perfect through his eyes.

Embrace yourself, people.
You are beautiful in every way.
Because you were made in His image,
Be thankful every day.

Listen!
...

How do you help someone
Who doesn't want to let go?

You can't.
No matter what obstacles are in their life
That keep them from a flow.

It's like a dam ready to break loose or a
Plane that's doomed for a crash landing or a
Boat that's sinking in the middle of the sea.

They say, "If only I had listened
To the spirit inside of me."

Know this, my brother and sister.
God wants you to be free—
Free from the stress of life.

You try to escape but you can't hide.

You need to let go of what is superficial
On the inside.

I know you are afraid of
What you may face ahead.

I know you are hurting inside.
Just pray and let God provide.

Quality of Life
...

Have you ever thought,
"It's not the quantity of life
But it's the quality of life that matters most?"

Do you live life to the fullest and try
To make each moment count?
Are you making a difference in the world?

Start with kindness
A sprinkle of love and
Fill it up with joy.

It will certainly make a difference
And will help change the world.

Generational Knowledge
...

Children are important in this society.
Remember, they are the next generation
When we pass from this life to the next.

Teach your children that money is made to survive.
But it's important to teach survival skills to maintain
In this life.

Teach them how God created the heavens and the earth.
And how He sent His son, Jesus Christ, to set us free.

Don't forget to teach them about respect.
It's a must in this society.

"Thank you" and "Please" are essentials.
Teach them to be grateful for what they have.

Teach them that family is important.

So, if you are happy about who you have become,
Let them know in your house,
This is not a democracy.
It's a dictatorship when it comes to the
Most important things in life.

Firefly, Firefly

Firefly, firefly,
Light up the sky.

Gazing and watching them
Flutter before my eyes.

They light up the trees;
They light up the grass before me.

Some glow in the water and
Some glow underground in burrows.

Yellow, orange and green,
They synchronize with their kind;
Fluttering their lights at night.

Firefly, firefly,
Light up the sky.

Fresh Start
...

Every day is a new journey
And a new beginning in life.

Take the opportunity each day
To get your life together.

Forgive someone if you need to.
Set new goals and achieve them.

Because tomorrow is a new day
And a new beginning.

Don't let it slip away.

One Hell of a Man
...

He was born a twin
From the fruit of his mother's womb.

He's 5'9" in stature and one hell of a man.
Born in Mississippi, raised in Michigan
In a little suburban town we call The Clem's.

Raised to be a Muslim and strong in his faith,
No liquor ever touched his lips
No cigarette to taste.

He's particular about what he puts in his body
No animal products for him.

His dad would sneak him into his place of employment
To teach him his trade.
It made a life impact on him
He was never the same.

He survived when life got hard,
But he never sat down.
He trusted in God to carry him through trials and tribulations
Because life never stops.

He was blessed with three children.
God added four more.
Married for 32 years to the beautiful Ms. Linda—
A strong, successful business woman that's for sure.

Now they have many grands and great grands too.
Twenty years with the Macomb Daily.
Twenty-five with the Detroit News.

He's still working, shoveling snow, and cutting grass too.
His motor is still running.
Thank God, because we adore him so.
Yes! He's 80 years old.

He's name is Farred.
And he's one hell of a man.

The Most High

...

I believe nothing happens by chance,
But it's predestined.

When I first moved into my condo,
It seemed that my neighbor was a nuisance
Consistently alerting us about parking in her space
When they should have parked in mine.
It's possible the feelings were mutual.

It was almost two years ago, before I found out
My neighbor was truly devoted to The Most High.

After losing someone special in my life,
I began to reach out more and more.

I realize I was sent here to this home,
Not by chance, but by The Most High.

He knew my love would not always be.
Therefore, He placed me in a safe place to comfort me.

I needed to change my lifestyle in more ways than one.

Tired of pharmaceuticals controlling my life.
I was introduced to certain foods I never tried or
Even heard of before.
To my surprise, I fell in love with the foods
God created for us.

She has led my family and friends
Out of the wilderness of unhealthy eating habits.

She is helping us get to a place
So our bodies can heal naturally.

If you follow her instruction,
You will get the best results.
No more pharmaceuticals can be your reward.

I have more stamina to run this race at a faster pace,
And parts of my body are falling in place.
We have taken control of our health and are
Trusting God to do much more.

My face is clear.
My skin is hydrated.
And the weight loss is sure enough a plus.

Teaching us how to make a change
Has been a challenge for some.
But, it's a lifestyle change.
Do you want to join us?

She is the sweetest neighbor and person
I wish everyone had.

Shall I call her Moses?
Shall I call her medicine woman?
Shall I call her an angel in disguise?

She's my neighbor,
Sent by The Most High.

In the Beginning
. . .

In the beginning,
God created man and gave him a plan.

He gave us nuts and berries, fruit and vegetables
And so much more than these to eat.

Herbs for healing our bodies and soul.
But everything changed
When man ventured off the road.

Labor pains for woman.
And the sweat of a man's brow
To survive in this world.

We have to reach back to
The beginning of God's plan.
Because sickness is alive in this land.

We have a choice He created for us.
I choose Life in the foods he created for us.

Not Death.

Rites of Passage

When you were born,
You were the center of our joy.

Just to know that God entrusted us
To give you back to him.
It was a huge responsibility for us.

At the age of ten,
You began to separate from us
Trying to create your own identity.

In your twenty's, you feel like a man,
Your mind expands in so many ways.

You think you have life all figured out, until
Life happens and causes you despair.

That's when you realize there's more to being a man.
And life is not as easy as you thought it was.

In your thirties, you search to find your place in life.
Wondering if you are on the right path
At this stage of your life.

In your forties, things happen beyond your control
You are realizing that nothing matters in this life
More than your relationship with God.

Peace and tranquility and doing what's right in God's eyes,
Is all you need to finish this race called life.

Finish the journey until God says it's time.
Just remember you're on the right track with God by your side.

So, don't beat yourself up because of the choices you made.

Be encouraged and know that God will love you always.

Just know that mothers will always love their sons,
No matter what.

Mothers are the second best—after God.

A Father's Heart

...

You're a father who carries your children in your heart.
Even though you are unable to express your love to them,
It doesn't mean you do not have a father's heart.

Each pump of your heart is an extension of the life that
You have given them to breathe...
And to be the person they are today.
This is something that no one can ever take away.

I know your heart longs to spend time with your children,
And that will come one day.

As for now, keep the faith and know, no matter what,
Continue to carry your children in your heart.

Faith has brought you a mighty long way.
That same faith will, in time, make a way.

Now, just believe that one day,
They will physically be a part of your life.
And remember they will always have your heart.

Duck!
...

Growing up with my brother,
He always terrorized and chased me.

One day, he put several gloves on his right hand
And punched me in my eye.

I ran to get away because
He just wouldn't stop chasing me.

Until one day mother said, "You better not cry or run
From your brother or else you will have to deal with me."
So, I had to stand up to my brother—or face my mother.

I looked at her and realized she was bigger than me.

He was a little terrorizing booger and
The highlight of his life was beating on me.

There was a big freezer right behind me. He took a swing.
I ducked like Muhammad Ali
And my baby brother
Punched the freezer instead of me.

He learned his lesson because
My brother no longer terrorized me.

Boon-Docks

. . .

My circle of friends from childhood to adulthood
I will never forget.
Some I've lost touch with through the years,
Only to cross paths with each of them again.
The memories are so precious to me.

One friend was always quiet,
But later she lost touch with reality.

One friend, we grew up together on Oakley St.
We played dolls until we were ten.

One friend always made quick decisions,
Only to regret them in the end.

One friend drove a little blue Pinto.
Of course we thought we were the junk back then.
Riding to Detroit and lying to our parents
About where we had been.
Down in the boon-docks...
We weren't very proud of living there then.

We lived through the Mt. Clemens High School riot of 1970.
Protesting because there was no racial equality in the city,
Let alone in the school system.

We lived through the assassinations of a few magnificent men.
They died for what they believed.
Malcolm X spoke the truth.
He wasn't afraid of any man.

Dr. Martin Luther King, Jr. fought against segregation
And led peaceful demonstrations,
And we see where that got him.

But look where we are now,
Only to have number forty-five
Trying to push us back again.

We were taken from our neighborhood elementary school
And were bussed to Selfridge Air Force Base.

We acted like misbehaving children.
Cussing like sailors.
Fighting like we grew up with no rules.
My mother straightened me out right away
By beating my behind over and over again.

We changed the dress code history
At George Washington Middle School.
We learned that we had a voice by sticking together, even then.

We survived many butt whippings.
It's a wonder we made it to adulthood.
The class of 1974, that's who we were.

Girls becoming mothers.
Their bodies just developed into womanhood.
Some became fatherless in their adolescent years.

I will never forget the tragedies
In the lives of my boon-dock friends.

We made it out of the boon-docks
And became productive people in society.

Man, what a ride!

I'll never forget the memories, but...
I wouldn't want to live them over again.

Eternal Rest

...

6:03 a.m. is when he took his last breath.
He left this earthly journey called life and
Landed in heaven's eternal rest.

No more pain.
No more sickness.
Free from the stress of life.

No regrets. He did his best.
He was a man of valor.
He was certainly put to the test.

He finished his work in this world,
By giving freely of himself.

Don't be sad.
Don't cry for him.
He's in eternity.

He's resting in peace.

Heart 2 Heart (In Memory of Pauletta)

The last time I remember setting my eyes
Upon your face (we embraced).

We took a moment and I could feel your pain
It will never be erased.

The pain of being tired of running this race.

Although I didn't know it would be the
Last time we saw each other face to face,

In that short moment,
We were saying "Goodbye."

I will never forget the connection we shared that day,
Through that warm heart 2 heart embrace.

I know it's not "Goodbye," but "See you later."

We will meet again in that heavenly sky.

If I Had Known
...

If I had known it was going to be my last time,
I would have said, "Goodbye."

If I had known it was going to be my last time,
I would have embraced you all night long.

If I had known it was going to be my last time talking to you,
I would have asked you more questions about
Everything that came to my mind.

Don't let it be the last time,
Without treating someone
As if it's your last time seeing them.

The Warrior
. . .

He was a warrior, strong and mighty
In the Lord.

He picked the toughest profession in life.
Walking into burning buildings to save lives.

He didn't complain.
He took life in stride.

He was a black man
Who went through some struggles in life.

He feared silently if he feared at all.

He was a great man. He stood very tall.

The knowledge that he gained was
Impeccable in every way.

In those last moments, I believe he said,
"Take me dear Lord, quickly today".

Are you a warrior such as he?
I pray for you to be someday.

Becoming Vegan
...

Becoming vegan is like
Being born again.

Your body begins to change
And to heal itself within.

Your brain becomes sharper
Like never before.

You wonder, why Lord didn't I do
This long before?

Why did it take so long to receive
The knowledge that you have given us long ago?

Because of man's lifestyle, we
Began to eat meat like carnivores.

We developed many sicknesses and diseases.
Now it's history.

Let's go back to the beginning of
How our God intended for us to eat.

It will save us from a lot of sickness and diseases.

He gave us everything we needed to survive on earth.

So, let's go back.

It surely won't hurt.

The Unsung Hero

...

After many days of ruminating within his soul...

The potential was always there, wrapped up inside.

He has awakened and is now in control.

He is that unsung hero, only a few really know.

Laden with talent, bursting to be free.

It has finally manifested from within his soul.

Now he has opened the door to receive so much more.

Archiving Memories

Archiving memories in my heart
Allows me to store those special moments
Inside never to part.

Safely archiving memories
Until it's less painful inside.

It helps to move forward,
Because life never stops.

It takes time, just wait and you will see.
Take my suggestion.
Archive those memories and you will succeed.

Give God complete control.
Let Him in. He wants your soul.

Please don't try to do this alone.
If so, it could take much longer than you realize.

No matter what stage of life you are in,
Archive just a little bit of your heart.
Don't be afraid of life or to
Let someone else in.

The Third Age

Sixty-five and I'm still alive with
More stamina than ever before.

Ready to take charge of my life
As God intended for me.

Feeling free as an eagle, flying high in the sky.

Lifestyle changes have a grip on me.
For all the better can't you see?

I'm ready to move forward with my life.
The journey is on for me.

Free as the waves moves swiftly across the sea.
No holds barred on me.

Just watch and see
All that my God has planned for me.

Spokes on the Wheel of Life
. . .

There are seasons in our lives
For a reason.

Sometimes the season becomes intolerable,
And you no longer want to deal with the pain.

So, you must make the decision to
Move on with your life.
Because the journey of the relationship must end.

Only then can growth take part
So you can survive.

Some seasons are long and some are shorter than most.

Only God knows what's in store
Concerning your journey.

But, you must be open to follow God's leading;
To be ready for the next season of the
Journey called Life.

Everlasting Prayer

How long shall I be upon this earth?

I want to fulfill the assignment that
You have set before me.

To spread love and kindness to
Everyone whose lives I touch.

To have patience and wait on You
Is what I want to do.

As I seek You, my desire is
A deeper walk with You.

To share the gifts and talents You have given me.
Prayerfully, I am using them to
Please You, My King.

As I go through each trial and test,
I will learn to have joy in the midst.

Chosen by Heart

...

She was only six days old as the story is told.
Now it's getting ready to unfold.

God sent an angel in my life for when I get old.
I met her when she was just under two,
Spoken into existence by her brother,
Who wanted a sister when he was only six years old.

Chosen by her father—he knew from the start,
That she would be the daughter to give of his heart.

Many years I spent to teach her about life.
She's a vivacious young lady and very bright.

She was sent by God from the start
To be a part of our ancestry on the family chart.

Now, all are grown and her oldest brother loves her too.

She's the girl who has captured our hearts.

God prepared the way for her from
The moment of conception.

She was chosen by God, to be our angel.
All because we opened our hearts.

Pearl
...

A pearl is a precious gem which comes from the sea,
But this Pearl came from South Africa to America
Searching for her destiny.

From salt water, the fresh water pearls
Are natural as they can be.
But nothing compares to the Pearl I know
That doesn't come from the sea.

Mother of all children, they flock to her on every side.

Yes! She is a precious gem
And I wouldn't trade her for anything
Because she means so much to me.

Blood Bond

. . .

She should have been my daughter...
She's so much like me.

Loud as she can be.
I think she's louder than me!

You can feel her energy when she
Comes through the door, and you
Will know, she's my niece.

We are both entrepreneurs
And determined as we can be.

We refuse to let anything take us down,
Because we don't clown around.

Her heart is truly tender to those she truly loves.

She's my niece and my protector.
She's always looking out for me.

She treats me like a precious dove.

She should have been my daughter...
She's a lot like me.

Quadripartite

I was told by my sister, Dottie, that
God gave us four rooms in our heart.

One for God, who supersedes all.

One for your spouse, which is
God's Plan from the start.

Don't forget the children.
They are room number three,
Which is His family plan.

Now, if for some reason
You lose that special person in your life,
God will show you that you can love again
If you open your heart.

My God is Brilliant

God created man in His own image.
Man thinks he is more brilliant than He.
I will tell you, that isn't true.

Man tries to make things better, but eventually,
The after effects create devastation.

It affects our nature of life that God intended a long time ago.

The air we breathe.
The water we drink.
The soil in which we plant our food.

Experimenting with all sorts of things which
Polluted our environment and it has
Cut man's lifespan on Earth.

God has a nature of life that is divine order and
That is the way things must go.

He is our Creator.
He is brilliant.

I told you so.

Joy, Real Joy

Joy, she's one of a kind.
Beautiful and vibrant in every way.

Just the sound of her name alone speaks
Volumes every day.

Our souls clicked from many years ago.
She helped me with a struggle that was a real tuggle.
Joy is genuine and one of a kind.

Real Joy can light up a room
And if you have tests and trials,
With Joy you will never be doomed.

Just pick up the word of God and find
Joy and peace within.

Joy is a fruit of the Holy Spirit.
Real Joy has blessed in her lifetime.

Her name sings praises to our King,
Which soothes our hearts and soul.

So, pick up a little Joy to get you through life's struggles
When the tests of life have come.

Proud Heritage
...

I am a product of my parents.
A strong heritage is where I came from.

Southern parents raised on a farm.
Feeding livestock, churning butter,
And planting everything on hand.

A little homemade wine...
My granddaddy used to take one sip at a time.

They had to plow the land in order to survive.

Daddy had some land that was
Passed down through generations.

He said, "Never sell it, especially not to the white man."

He said, "This is all I have. Protect it. I know you can."

It's been 18 years and
I'm still holding on to
That six acres of land.

My Heart Belongs to Africa
...

Africa has been in my heart since 1984.
That was the year I met my dear friend, Ransome,
Who came from East Africa.

Intrigued by the drummers,
Fascinated with the movements of their feet.
While dancing, they tell a story.

The style of their clothing is colorful and uniquely designed.
All of this gives me a connection to my ancestors.

These are the symbols that remind me that
I am made up of different regions
All across the world.

I am...
43% Nigeria.
26% Cameroon.
Congo and part of southern Bantu people, too.
18% Mali.
3% Senegal.
10% of other regions.
Which is mixed with Ireland, Scotland, Norway, Ghana, Portugal
And Spain, too.
Now my ethnicity has been established.
I am so colorful and free.

I am proud to be part of the Motherland
From whence I've come.

My heart and soul belong to Africa.
Especially when I hear the beat of the drums.

My skin is black.
My head is bald.
My nose is wide.
My curves remind me that I fit in.

So, no matter where I came from,
Africa or America,
I am proud to be me and
Proud to be free.

My heart belongs to Africa.

The Comforter
...

My heart aches some mornings and nights.
Oh! How I miss my true love.

The thought of not having my love physically with me;
He's still in my heart.

Nothing or no one can ever replace my loss.
With time the pain becomes lighter.

As I stretch out my faith from day to day,
The Holy Spirit—my Comforter—
Reminds me of His
Precious and holy word.

As I give praises daily to Christ my King,
I'm singing, "Hallelujah, hallelujah! Praise God!
Thank You for comforting me."

Conception
...

Imagination as a child is everything.
Imagination as an adult is important as well.

If you suppress one's ability to imagine
It can stun their creativity.

Wealthy people imagined and dreamed
Until they achieved their success.

Encourage the imagination by allowing
One to explore their creativity.

The Front Row
...

Everyone gets a turn
To sit on the front row.

It doesn't matter who you are, or
Who you have become.

Everyone gets a turn
To sit on the front row.

The question is:
How will you handle life
When it's your turn to
Sit on the front row?

Sibling Squabbles

We are sisters
Made from the same bloodline.

Born generations apart,
Sometimes I don't know where to start.

Reaching out again and again
Trying to understand.

Why do we have so many
Obstacles that keep us apart?

We must let the past go, or else
The devil will take control.

Life is too short.

Let it go!

A Little Bit of Heaven (Trim Pines)

...

As I searched and searched for a place to
Spend my birthday weekend,
I came across a little place called Trim Pines.

As I approached this little place,
It felt like a little bit of heaven to me.

I believe being in the presence of God is like
Soaking up all that He created within the land
And the trees—between the heavens and the earth.

The birds are chirping and singing in the morning dew.

To see the leaves swiftly moving in the breeze.
Oh! How peaceful to walk the gravel and the grass
Between the trees created with such
Splendor and beauty to behold.

I can see butterflies, moths and the bees
Doing what they need to do beneath the trees.

I can see and hear nature all around.
The geese, horses, squirrels, and rabbits too.

"A little bit of heaven,"
In search of,
Inside of me,
Called Trim Pines.

True Gem
...

Strong, determined, feisty, and particular
Is what I see in her.

A looker, a dresser and
Some people call her "boujee"
Is what I've gleaned from her.

Direct, responsible and always helped her family.
Caring for all.
Like her is how I want to be.

A true gem is she.

Ancestral Heritage
. . .

There she is.
The land that my forefathers purchased long ago
To give to their children and children's children
As a heritage to work and live on.

A tiny little house with only a few rooms to share,
But yet they all got along.

Fourteen children plus one more,
But never in the house at the same time.

All of them ventured north where other family members
Paved the way, except two, plus one more.
They were seeking their destiny.

They became farmers, automakers, nurse assistants,
Household technicians and beauticians.
They were honest and loved each other so.

They taught us that family was important
By gathering regularly.

Yes! That is the land in Mississippi that
We hold so dear to our hearts.
To me, it's the land of the free.

Our forefathers kept alive in us through their children
And children's children.

Please catch the vision for your children.

Church Family

I believe everyone should have a church family.
No matter what happens,
They are always there.

To hold your hand when you're feeling down.
To offer prayer when the need is there.

If you feel lonely, just find a church family.
Especially when your family
Is no longer there.

Global Pandemic of 2020
...

It was the winter of 2020
When the pandemic hit the world.

No place to hide, not even inside.
Your groceries and mail could be infected as well.

Businesses folded, jobs lost, schools closed.
Education for our children suffered.
How much?
Only time will tell.

People working from home.
Parents falling apart
Because they have to teach their own.

Grandparents dying, leaving grandchildren without
That word of wisdom to help them sprout
Because they had illnesses that compromised their health.
This virus has taken control.

The government provided extra help, so a lot of
People made more money by sitting on their tails.

It's a terrible parasite. They call it Covid-19.

Weddings and events cancelled.
Hospitals taking precautions and
Only emergency surgeries were performed.

Supplies are in demand; deliveries at a standstill.

Wash your hands. Wear your mask. Don't touch your face.
Don't go in crowds. No hugs or kisses.

Yes! We are starving from the human touch
Which affects our mental health as well.
Gas prices at their lowest, but nowhere to go.
People are praying that Corona won't hit their door.

We call it a pandemic, a plague, a parasite or Covid-19.
Whatever the name, it has no respect of persons.
Young or old, rich or poor.
Black or white.
Jewish or Hispanic, Asian and many more.

It's so important to know where you are going
When you leave this world.

I'm praying that you don't wind up in hell.

Essential Rules

...

I am not understanding why people wait hours
After rising to the floor to do what is necessary
Before they hit the door.

Living alone or with someone else,
Trust me you can't ignore.

Brush your teeth! They look a mess!
I can see the yellow plaque has taken residence.

So please don't slack.
Hurry up and take care of that!

Pick it, floss it, use some Listerine if you must
To rinse those particles out of your breath.
Two days later is not what's best.
Your dragon breath breathes fire.
It's a mess and please don't put me to the test.

Bathing is essential.
It's an important rule for humans.

Comb your hair and please get dressed.
That's a routine that should not be missed.

Wash your feet and clip those toe nails, ears and nose hairs.
You might as well. It's no excuse.
Hire someone to do it.
People get paid to clean up a neglected mess.

After you pee pee, flush the toilet please!
I don't want bubbles hitting my stuff.

If you move your bowels check to see what residue
You might have left.

Please wash your hands after each use so your
Fingers don't smell like cow poo.

These are the skills that will help you through.
I call them essential rules.
It will make all of our lives easier—
It's for the best.

The Chambers of Eve's Heart
...

I make no apologies for who I am,
Because God created me.
To be Sunshine when the rain is
Falling in several spots around me.

I make no apologies for who I am
Because God created me.
I am flamboyant as I can be.
I hope you can see.

I am liberated in my thoughts, so
Don't try to imprison me
Because a long time ago,
My God rescued me.

I make no apologies for who I am.
Just accept me,
Because God created me.

Spring in the Southern Hemisphere
...

Apologies are like flowers that bring
Healing to the soul.
Before someone closes their eyes,
It's a sweet gift I'm told.

It is sweet and also savory that
Lingers within a soul.

Let not the mind forget the good memories
That saturate within.

It bubbles over us and absorbs all the
Beauty in our childhood to adulthood
That won't let us leave behind.

The root is the strength
That holds the stem and the petals of life.

As we give it nutrients within the soil—
Water and sunshine, it will need to survive.

By feeding this flower, it will blossom
Into wisdom and beauty as it should.

It was just tucked away.
It was always inside.

It is wisdom that brings beauty to the
Flower of life.

Accumulator

I am unable to comprehend
Why people become hoarders.

Is it the past you don't want to rid yourself of?

Clothes piled up high, almost to the sky.
Your basement packed with multiple items
You don't use.

No place to lay your head on your bed,
Because the clothes have taken control.

At some point you must let things go.
Make a decision to come face-to-face
With the real issue at hand.

So you can have deliverance before your life ends.

Hoarding is a sickness,
Please understand.

The Wings of Championship
...

Turbulence on a plane
Is no fun at all.

Turbulence in your life
Can be a lot of strife.

Praying that the unstable
Rough ride ahead
Will come to a smooth
Landing instead.

Going through
You don't know what to do.

Just study the course
And be calm.

Before you know it,
You will get through.

Study the course.
Don't look back.

The gain is rewarding for you.

In My Mother's Dwelling
. . .

I can feel the presence of our ancestors
When our families gather around.

I can visualize a smile upon
The countenance of their faces.

They were faithful to one another
And they pitched in whenever they could.

They shared a bond and
All of us share the same bloodline.

We were taught good hospitality rules.

When we were children
Our families would come from miles around
And they would stay awhile.

Hotels were never an option.
A couch, a pallet on the floor,
A bed or even the bathtub made
A cozy hub.

We always made room at the Inn
Because being together was
The most important to them.

The family spreads on the table
Had food of every kind.
No one complained about who didn't contribute.
They were just happy that you were around.

First cousins, second, third or fourth...
All we ever knew is that
We were family and
That's what we were told.

Cousins outside playing.

Back then, television was the only distraction
To keep us from creating a bond.

Some of us have lost our parents,
Grandparents, uncles, aunties
And siblings too.

One thing I believe is that
Cousins will always be there for you.

Now this is what our parents taught us
They are good rules.

Now tell me,
What level of hospitality do you give?

Please.
Don't break your parents' rules.

Wajukuu (Grandchildren)
...

Grandchildren are a blessing from God.
But most of the little darlings have been spared the rod.

Destructive to your furniture and
Marks on your walls.

Stepping over people;
Butting into conversations.
In my day, it wasn't heard of at all.

Teach them to give up their seat
When an adult is present.

And how to choose their words very carefully.

Teach them while they are still young, to
Uphold the truth and
Not to defend wrong.

Help them to understand that
Each chastisement is a lesson learned.

Then pray for mannerable, God-fearing children.
And pray that they will
Teach their children the same as well.

Irresistible
...

Your beard is a magnet
To my fingers.

I love to run my fingers through it.

I can see the curls and gray hairs
Bursting through it.

It makes you look very distinguished.

I know it tickles when I run my fingers through it.
You always say, "Don't do it!"

Every time you pat it down,
I take my hand and constantly do it.

Because your beard is a magnet
To my fingers...
I am going to continue to do it.

A Butterfly Trapped in Honey

You say you love me,
But I can't tell.

It's more than
Hugs and kisses
Planted all over my face.

You say you love me,
But I can't tell.

It's more than
Whispering
Sweet words in my ear.

It's more than
A few gifts
You have given to me.

I cannot teach you how to
Love me.
It's much too stressful for me.

Communication is the key.
But unless it's comprehended,
It's of no value to me.

It hurts that
You can't tell how much
I loved you.

With my actions,
I showed you in detail how much
I cared.

You say you love me,
But I can't tell.
I think you're stuck in your own world.

Hurt by many can be a
Cause and effect
To keep love from being a
Part of our lives.

One day, you might realize
How to love me.
By then it will be too late.

The journey is over, and
I believe you feel it as well.

Sometimes
Love is not enough
To build a life together.

It takes giving and receiving
Across the board.

I believe I spoiled you.
I think, beyond repair.

If we are meant to be together,
Only time will tell.

A Father's Ballad

I loved you from the first moment
I felt you though your mother's womb.

It was a struggle for you to come
Through the passage of life;
To breathe in the breath of this earth's air.

I held onto you until I took my last breath.

Even though I can't physically
See you wed this day,
I always knew you would make a way.

I can see you through your mother's eyes.
What's in her heart is also in mine,
Because we were one until
Death we parted.

You have become the man I knew you would be.
With just a little push to get a fresh start from me.

Now you have a special person
Who is the beat of your heart,
As your mom was mine.

We pray that you love her to the end of time.
Like the twelfth of never, and that's a very long time.

These are the words that I would say
If I was there.

"Well done, my son. And always remember,
I'm just a beat away, within your heart."

Transitioning
...

Watching your loved one
Transitioning
From life to death.

Starry eyes, focused on the walls,
You see depression upon their face.

One day they come face to face with the
Reality of death.
Knowing that true life
Is on the other side.

They make peace with their Maker—
The One who has
The power of life and death.

Then they realize
We are only here for just a short while.

You being that loved one who goes to
Your heavenly father for assurance;
To remind you, it will be alright.

Don't be selfish.
Let them go, so they can be free.

Even though they won't be near,
The memories you shared will
Always be there.

Wisdom from Persephone
...

It's the simple things in life
That bring pleasure to me
In my sixties.

Watching the flowers bloom
And listening to the birds sing,

Observing the sun
Bursting through the heavens looks
Brand new, while feeling the
Mist of the dawn dew.

Staring at rocks.
Gazing at the water.
Waves in the ocean.
Watching the children play at the park.
People passing through.

Living life to the fullest,
Is what I want to do.

Spreading love and joy...
I hope it reaches to you.

I Am That Woman

I am not
A genie stuck in a bottle
Waiting for someone to let me out.

I am not
A flower that never blooms.

I am not
A caterpillar stuck
In the chrysalis stage of life.

Nor an egg that will never hatch.

I am that woman,
Who will not be contained,
But has to be free.

I am like
A perennial that
Springs up every year
Without being replanted,
Because the joy of life
Is always within me.

I am that butterfly
That went through different stages of life
In order to be free.

I am the egg that hatched and
Became all that she could be;
Waiting to explore
All that life has to offer me.

I am that woman.

Love Incarnate
...

He is a gem that was found in
A treasure box
That no one else had discovered before.

Raised by strong Christian parents
That refused to let him go, until he
Faced life lessons and followed the
Straight and narrow road.

Love, patience, and understanding
Is what she saw in him.

Her knight in shining armor
She was always searching for.

Her black beauty is so graceful and
Her heart is pure.

She was raised so beautifully by her parents.
She is the jewel
Shining bright as the stars in heaven;
Glowing in the night above the trees.

Her heart is like a precious lamb.
She's sweet as a honeycomb
Attached to a tree.

Her strength to conquer all in prayer
Who were in disbelief.

No one had discovered the qualities
In her before.

I do believe God turned their eyes away,
So they couldn't see the beauty
She possessed inside her being.
Nor his potential that was
Waiting to be released.

Because God preserved them for each other,
He heard her prayer and his plea.
So, God pruned and plucked him very quickly.

He was ready to be steadfast.
Faithful.
Committed.
The man God intended for him to be.

They have rescued one another
By loving each other unconditionally.

Now they are one,
As God planned them to be.

Expressions of a Poet

Poetry is an expression
Of what lives within.

At some point
The words trickle out
To visualize and observe
What life is all about.

It is an array of thoughts that
Sometimes you can't even talk about

Who dare challenges the poet
That releases the ink from the pen?

It becomes the instrument to help
You release everything that's
Bottled up from your inner being.

Splatter of words that sprinkle
All over the page
Just to be heard.

Now they are exposed
For everyone to absorb.

I hope you enjoy the magic of the pen
That screams to be discovered and heard.

Poets write poetry as an expression
To release their feelings
In order to be free.

Too many are bound in this society.
Take some time to express yourself...

Try a little through poetry.

Love Prevails

. . .

I woke up this morning with a
Question on my mind:
What if God quit on me?

How would I react?
What would I do?
Would I pray more?
Would I read His word more?
Would I stop knocking at His door?

Would I feel hurt and unwanted?
Alienated? Or that
He turned His back on me?

This is what we do to Him when
We refuse to recognize the sacrifice
He made by sending His only
Begotten Son to set us free.

He showed us how much he loved us.

Now, what are we going to do?

Praise Him.
Pray to Him.
Talk to Him
He wants a relationship with you.

He hasn't forgotten.
He made a promise.
He is true to His word.

Are you?

Cabaret Waltz
...

Romance hasn't changed.
It's the same now as it was back then.

Men are visual creatures.
Someone catches his eye and he pursues her.

And he generally knows what to do.
A dozen roses or a card or two.

A poem, or a few sweet words might do.
If you'll be creative, she'll love that too.

Valentine's Day or any day,
You should remind her that
Your love is true.

Now don't forget to show you care.
Don't get too busy that you forget she's there.

Don't be stingy,
Especially if she's not stingy with you.

Now remember the romance you started
You must continue to do.

Especially if she reminded you, and you
Want her love forever and
Your dear heart is true to you.

You must romance her to keep her
And make sure it never ends.

Remember romance hasn't changed.
It is up to you.

Infinite Love

There is not a day that goes by
That I don't think of you.

Sometimes I shed a few tears
Because I miss you.

Wondering what heaven will be,
Like when God calls me home too.

We were so full of love and life
Since the time I met you.

Throughout our journey together
Almost a half century of memories
To commemorate upon.

We shared joy and tears
Within those years.

We travelled many miles to different destinations.

Africa.
Puerto Rico.
Hawaii.
And coasting on the sea shores to
Different islands and
Parts of the United States too.

Far and near,
By car, plane, train.

It was a pleasure to be your Queen.
And you were my King,
During our season of life here on earth with me.

There is not a day that goes by that
I don't remember how much you loved me
And I loved you.

Reckoning
...

The core in the center of my heart
Feels as if it had been ripped apart
When I hear someone dehumanize another person.

Words that cannot be taken back
Are put into the atmosphere
To roam the world and take form.

A body used as a human punching bag.
God paid the price—you shouldn't have to.

Taking someone's life over strife.
Is it worth it to trade your life?

Someone being ravished
Because of what was done to them.

This is called "dehumanizing" in one of the worst forms.
They want to rob you of your body and soul,
So they can take control.

It makes me nervous on the inside and
Shake on the outside.

It's scary when a person has checked out on a sane life.
They are stripping themselves
more than they are stripping you.

Remember, you have no right to
Make someone's life a living hell.
That is Satan's job. Don't let him use you.

No one should suffer abuse or zap life out of you.

The last I read, God has a record of everything you do.
On judgement day it will be waiting for you.

We all have a choice.
Repent and become brand new.

We can't fool God.
He knows our heart.
Whether you are for real or
Just playing a temporary part.

Tiara the Fascinator
...

She is an heirloom.
Many have worn her
Throughout the years.

She's sparkly and beautiful,
With two combs to hold her hair.

Bridal showers, birthdays, and weddings—
They all adore her and she loves to attend.

Many would love to wear her or
Just to try her on.

She's an heirloom.

She is beautiful—
Tiara the Fascinator.

House of Haven

This is a house that I have made a haven.
It's what God gifted me.

Where people come from miles around
Just to lay their head.

I set my table so they may feast on a good meal.
It is a blessing for me as well.

When they leave my home,
I make sure they feel as if
Jesus had been served there.

All who walk into my haven,
I'm sure they are not the same.

Because, God has anointed me the blessing;
Sharing my haven when I can.

I will feed all who walk through my doors,
Although I don't have much.
But I have the greatest gift God gave me
And it's called Love.

Journey of My Weight in Time

This poem is not about you, but about my truth.
If you ever struggled with weight,
I know you can relate.

Our eating habits are learned behavior
From our parents and each generation before.

It takes time to reverse those behaviors.
But you have to gain knowledge to fight the war.

Meat, dairy and sugar is very good, but it takes
Re-educating one's self to realize
You don't need all of that to survive.

Overweight can be debilitating to your body and soul.

Three hundred pounds of flesh and bones
Pulling and tugging and weighing me down.

The struggle was real!

I never tried fad diets because after the weight loss,
You have to gain control over what you feed
Your body and soul.

I remember when the tape measure was
Too short to go around my butt.

To get on a horse was way too much.
I'm sure it was tragic for the horse and for me.

In 2009, medical weight loss was the key for me.
I was on a journey. I lost one-hundred pounds and I
Felt free. I gained forty back.

I told you the struggle was real!

Over the past ten years, I've learned a lot
To help myself figure out what it's all about.

Giving up meat these last few years
Improved my health
And I learned how to eat.

Never thought beans, mushrooms, fruits and vegetables
Would be for me.

I shall not go back...
I have been set free!

Now being able to wrap a towel around my body
Is a dream come true.

Being able to see between my thighs
When I touch my toes...
I never realized how much that would please me so.

I can get off the floor
Without making a scene.

And sit on a plane without my thighs
Touching the person beside me.

I can walk more than a mile
And stay on the elliptical for quite a while.

Now the struggle is still real!

I just can't miss days without being on the scale.
Because that is the reality that never lies and
It looks you in the face every time.

The most important lesson is to realize
You are beautiful at any size.

I'm mesmerized at what God has done.
You can do it too.
If you trust Him, He will help you through.

Just be true to yourself and
Never let anyone steal your joy from you.

Whether it's about your weight,
Your hair,
Your looks,
Your feet,
Your hands,
Your lips,
Or whatever someone may say to be cruel to you...

Just remember you are loved by God and
You just have to love yourself too.

Message to My Sistahs
. . .

I often wonder if I can really love again
Or even have a special friend.

I believe I can, but the chances are very slim.

I am a well-balanced, seasoned woman,
That most can't understand.

I know my worth and how I should be treated
And expect nothing less than.

Some call me spoiled and that's a fact.
If opening a car door and carrying a few bags is being spoiled,
Then so be it.

I thought gentlemen are supposed to do that.
I believe they think chivalry is dead.

It's true I have spoiled a few friends
To the point they expect it.

But when it's time to reciprocate,
They can't understand, and
They wonder why I choose to walk away.

I will not allow someone to play games
By putting me through tests.

I have offered my kindness and support
And they offer me a $20 bill.
I want to know what's up with that?

Some have issues that have spiraled out of control.
They are so stuck in their ways
And they can't see past their pain.

I have met a few men past the age of sixty-five.
It seems like most of them are

Happy with their lazy boy recliners
And big screen TV's, waiting for eternal rest.
Some are very handsome
With curly hair down their back.

But I hope they know
It takes more than that.

I believe too many women
Have told them they are the prize.

However, my opinion is consistant.
They got it twisted.
Remember my "sistah," YOU are the prize!

Listen young ladies, don't settle for less.
There's nothing golden about them
That you have to put up with their mess.

A friendship/relationship is about giving and receiving,
Not take, take, take.

Learn to love on yourself.
You don't need a male friend to do that.

My standards might be high.
I say, "Why not?"

I pray this poem may help you in life,
Especially if he whispers sweet nothings in your ear,

Take heed my sistah.
You can't survive off of that.

When you go into a relationship,
Make sure you have something to offer as well.

If you don't have it together, get it together.
A prepared King is looking for a prepared Queen.

A Tribute to Mama Whiteside

...

I called her Mama.
Yes! She's a mother indeed.

Outspoken, beautiful and sassy
In her own way.

Since I've known her,
Her spirit has always been the same.

She was one of several people
That prayed for my soul.

I was on the front line
Ready for a firing squad
To be taken down
Because the devil was taking control.

God moved her to intervene
With prayer and fasting.

I heard his voice and answered the call.
He saved my soul once and for all.

I've never forgotten the love she showed.

Our relationship has deepened
Over the past few years.

Our visits are a blessing to me
And I am sure to her as well.

I never had a mother that
I could share my deepest thoughts with.

God placed her in my life
To fill a void in my heart.

Her name is Mama Whiteside and
I cherish her.

She's a prayer warrior.
A strong pillar in the community.
A mother to the motherless.
A friend to the friendless.
An advisor and a good listener, too.

At the age of eighty-nine she gets around better than me
And probably you, too.

Dear God,
Thank you for Mama Whiteside.
I pray You continue to
Give her more strong and healthy years.

Until You say,
"Well done, My faithful servant."

Life Ingredients

What is life?

It's about a little bit of this
And a little bit of that.

It's about love and hate, life and death,
Comfort and pain, war and peace.

It's about sunshine in the midst of the rain.

It's about sorrow, joy and laughter, power,
Conflict, confusion, experience, wisdom, and growth.

Life is about survival and
Learning to pick up your life after the pain.

It's about being alone and
The seasons in our lives that brings a change.

It's about having freedom to make your own choices,
Whether they are right or wrong.

It's about growing older, losing your hair and
Dealing with trials and tests at any age.

It's about networking and learning to work together
To achieve a common goal.

It's about being courteous and kind;
Truth and trust.

Life is about family, and teaching our children
How to survive in this world.

Being accepted, believing in yourself,
In sickness and health.

Life happens no matter who you are or where you're from.

As I said, "It's about a little bit of this and a little bit of that."

Just keep living.
That's life.

Essence of a First Lady

A first lady knows how to dress without being provocative.
It's about having class and knowing how to carry herself.
She builds her empire and does not tear it down.
She's polite and elegant in her own special way.

She's hospitable, zealous,
And embraces life from day to day.
Her personality causes people to flock to her side.
Her smile is contagious and her word is her bond.

She has talents that allow her to achieve
All that she put her hands to.
She has fears but she never lets them hold her down.
She has grace and royalty like a peacock.
Friendly as a capybara.
Confidence like a moose.
The strength of a panther.
And the courage of a lion.

She has worn multiple hats in her lifetime.
She has stood through the storms
In the dfferent seasons of her life
And always comes through
Shining like a Sakura diamond.

She has control over her temper.
Giving and showing love are her best qualities
Because of her love for her God.

She is the pure essence of a first lady,
With a lot of class.

My Pen, My Paper, My Poetry

What would I do without my pen
To write about my experiences and the world I live in?

What would I do without my paper
To write down my thoughts to clear my head?

What would I do if I didn't have a heart
To share my love with the people I care for?

What would I do if I didn't have my poetry
To share with all of you?

Words of wisdom and compassion
To capture what is deep within my heart.

About the Author

...

Doris Dean Hannah Turner is a gifted and multi-talented entrepreneur. Her credits include "Dolls Exquisitely Dressed by Doris" which were featured and showcased in numerous Detroit Public Schools. She is one of the co-founders of "Lady Butterflies," a girls' mentorship program at Chandler Park Academy.

God has breathed life into her ideas and given her courage to follow through as an entrepreneur. Doris' interests include traveling, shopping, cooking, meeting family, and making people laugh.

She earned a Certificate in Ministry from the California School of Ministry. She later earned her certification in rules of etiquette behavior from "The Etiquette Institute" in St Louis, MO.

The author of "An African Rock: Sacred Poems of Love, Loss, Legacy & Life" (2020) Doris is one of the writers of the anthology, "A Widow's Resilience: Wisdom Keys for Moving Forward in Life and Love After Death Do Us Part" (2021).

Contact the Author:

Email: turnerdd62@gmail.com
Facebook: @doris.hannahturner
Facebook: @An-African-Rock-656810391601722
Instagram: @dorishannahturner

www.ingramcontent.com/pod-product-compliance
Lightning Source LLC
Chambersburg PA
CBHW050302120526
44590CB00016B/2460